CONVERSATION WITH SILENCE

Evincepub Publishing

Nehru Nagar, Bilaspur, Chhattisgarh 495001
First Published by Evincepub Publishing 2021
Copyright © Satish Vimal 2021
All Rights Reserved.

ISBN: 978-93-5446-125-5

CONVERSATION WITH SILENCE

Satish Vimal

Translated by: Ashraf Raavi

<u>A litterateur's Diary</u>

Conversation with Silence

ISBN: 978-93-5446-125-5

Price: Year of Publication: 2021

'I tell myself to myself and throw the burden on my book and feel relieved'

......**Anne Lister**

'I always say, keep a diary, and someday it will keep you'

......**Mae West**

'Many people hear voices when no one is there. Some of them are called mad and are shut up in rooms where they stare at the walls all day. Others are called writers and they do pretty much the same thing'

......**Meg Chittenden**

To all those who hear voices from silence...... To all those who carry their own measuring rods with them....... To all those whom people call mad or the writers...

To my father who lives within me

**To Jalaal Sahib who wrote me and
made me write**

What made me translate the diary?

The dismal condition of the literary quality in our language in conjugation with the emergence of countless poets (without having even faded- trace of poetic quality) and non-serious flat prose writers has suffocated a number of genuine poets, writers and critics. However, the presence of genuine living poets and adequately worthwhile prose writers cannot be ruled out but they are only a few. Such a condition of our language is not the outcome of merely what I say but it is also because of the mushroom growth of literary organisations. The outcome of these literary organisations is not more than holding *Mushairas* (poetic symposiums), recital of praising articles devoid of any critical analysis and compromising mutual conferring of awards and titles. These things are rampant in our literary era and no one raises his voice against it other than *Satish Vimal* who could not restrain himself and record his observations in his diary. He published a part of the dairy under the title "Litterateur's dairy", the first of its kind written in Kashmiri language. It is the inclusive critical analysis of our dismal literary condition in it that inspired me to translate the same into English. It is also because my literary taste and knowhow intersects somewhere with that of Satish Vimal's and resultant angle engulfs not only we two but so many of the like- minded fellows who are non-vocative or mum well-wishers of the language and culture.

Satish Vimal's diary is an elaborate logical critical analysis of contemporary literature and literary scenario. It is without ambiguities and compromises and these qualities render it the characteristics of theory in Kashmiri criticism. As such the dairy is to be read and analysed for correction of taste and standard in literature. The motive for turning it into English is to widen its reach to varied horizons.

Ashraf Raavi

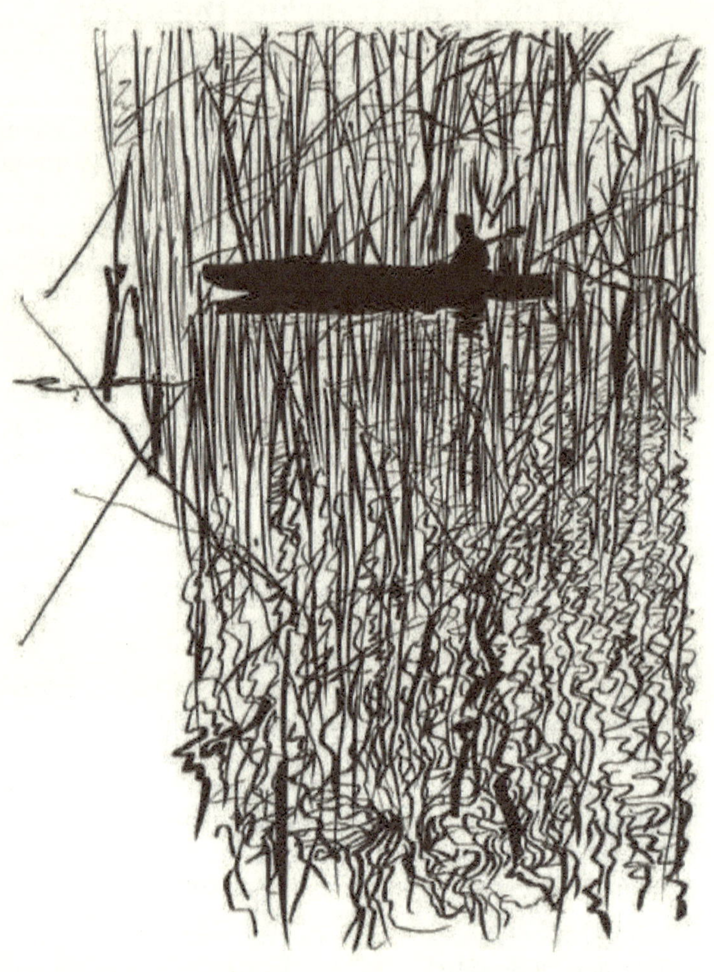

X

Preface

A writer learns to write while writing. The ability of giving life to his creation develops in him only after passing over so many challenging psychological speed breakers. As in every trade a man attains perfection gradually, in the same way the art of writing literature perfects day by day and as such the skill is developed.

There isn't any specific and set rule for creating a better literary work. A writer's themes are the creations and delineations of his mind and his style is an image of his character and nature. That is why Robert Pen Warren writes, "True writers are those who want to write, who need to write and hence write"

On visiting a blank paper and gazing towards it, a writer's third eye opens on his forehead. In the light of the third eye he observes the new world and sees what he cannot see by his two physical eyes. Later he records his observation on the blank paper. After writing, he says, "I wrote because I had to write and if you have to write, then write; not writing isn't any option".

I was a little chap when my grandfather, who had mastery on so many languages and branches of knowledge, was writing his diary for half an hour or an hour daily in the evening. Later when I was able to hold a pen in my hand, I also started writing a diary. I wrote a number of diaries and kept pleasing myself in reading them. On certain times I felt ashamed and on others I experienced an ecstasy in it. By and by the nature of my diary changed. Now there were so many pages in the diary which I wanted to be listened to or read by a person other than me. Now the diary had not remained of me alone but it was like my poetry turning to be of one and all. This feeling encouraged me to select some pages and put them in the hands of readers. Whether my courage was reasonable or not, it would be known when the critical and wise readers will give their opinions.

Satish Vimal

9 August 2008

I found fifteen years old edition of the famous Urdu journal *'Nayi Duniya'* in the library of one of my acquaintances when I visited him. We were having a friendly talk after so many years when my glances fell on the interview of a famous Hindi writer *Mahadevi Verma* published in it. One of the questions of the interviewer was: "The sensibility has been reducing continuously in every sphere of life. The humour and fun don't seem entertaining now. What can be done in such a condition?" *Mahadevi's* reply was: "It is certainly a sorrowful condition but there isn't anything to worry about. The wheel of time keeps moving on always. Nowadays the immorality and filth has erupted upwards. Very soon all this vice would get dumped underneath and all the virtue would erupt upwards. Nobody can stop the movement of the wheel of time."

On reading this I recollected *Ved Vyas*. Even a very famous learned scholar, writer and spiritually uplifted person, *Ved Vyas* had to say, while struggling with the unfavourable conditions, "Nobody listens to me. I should perform my duty honestly and I should wait as well till the turn of good days." Today it is the duty of writers that they should not let the lofty head of humanity and art droop. When a writer sells his conscience, the world entangles in filth and dross. The text of the interview of *Mahadevi Verma* published a number of years before is still relevant because even today there is a need for constructive freedom of expression for living in dignity. We should courageously defunct all those influences which blunt our pen and tongue, which constraint our freedom of observing, listening, thinking and speaking.

This struggle is very old but new, novel and contemporary in every situation as well. We are living in such an era, the unfortunate reality of which is that writers produce ephemeral literature and go commercial. This condition gives way to such a business of loss in which we ceremoniously sing for the 'prostrate-mentality' for getting hollow applause and recognition. This nonsense ceremonial singing itches the heart and makes a wise man uncomfortable and sleepless. Isn't it better to be in the slumber of ignorance than to be in such nonsense and futile but apparently an auspicious and augured deed?

24 August 2008

Today early in the morning at his residence at *Udaywala* in Jammu, *Arjun Dev Majboor* recited to me some stanzas from a long poem of an ancient poet. I was there to visit him. By the way we started talking about the evolution of the era or rather about the turn of the era and its impact on the literary expression. Mr Majboor recited to me the Hindi translation of a Chinese poem. The poet had talked about the theme (we were talking about) beautifully with the help of metaphors. Then I remained involved within the same theme throughout the day. The procession of varied attitudes kept going along with me the whole day and when in the evening I sat lonely in the hotel trying to comfort myself, the echoes of the procession were recurrently with me.

On one hand it is being sed that as everything changes in the world, the change in the relations of humanity and love cannot be ruled out and the delineation of these relations that is literature can't be static. On the other hand, it is being said that human nature and desires are unaltered right from the primordial time. Nothing changes in them nor is it possible in future because the roots of human conduct are so deep that superficial winds can't change them.

In between these paradoxical ideas, a number of mental attitudes take birth and a new condition emerges before the eyes. One condition is that even if human conduct and goodness would not change but the nature and forms of expression change necessarily. Another condition is that when everything changes from within, its impact is felt by us in outward manifestation of conduct as well. Otherwise, the condition is that between the previous two conditions there is an ever-changing antithetic relation despite it being said or thought that nothing has changed. When a human try to put constraints and halts in the way of change, and on the other hand when a man keeps aloof from his past on thinking that everything has changed, there and then the unchanging elements of human conduct and goodness take hold of him again. All these rather all other relatable facets and attitudes have been presented in our literature right from the times of *Lalla Ded*. Nowadays when the era is impregnated with the scientific revolutions and market influences, the strong need is felt to write on these attitudes.

16 November 2009

Today I saw one of my teachers. I felt happy on seeing him but my teacher seemed happier than me on meeting me. I felt very humble and my whole body drenched in sweat when I heard him saying, "I am proud of my students like you." He treated me with due respect although in reality it was he who was to be highly respected because he had taught me and guided me. I recollected his number of lectures which he used to deliver on morning assembly in the school. We used to nickname him as 'the noble creations' because he would often use this word in his lectures to inspire us to become good human beings. The pleasure of meeting the respectable teacher, I still feel. However I think that perchance I would have become a litterateur but it is impossible for me to become the noblest of the creations.

Man had been dreaming of being the centre of power since he stepped on the first rung of the ladder of progress. Gradually he forgot that this world hadn't been created merely for him. He forgot that an ant or any other miniature insect is equally entitled to the earth as he is. It is unfortunate that human beings started eroding those bases on which he was dignified as the noblest and the most beautiful of the creations. The illusions of being powerful made him rise against himself. He thinks, "As everything in the universe is subjugated by me then what is the challenge to my lordship." The poison of this idea dispersed throughout the existence of the human being and he murdered his own brother for merely a *marla* of land and as such it was the beginning of the bloody history of human beings. This illusion of power manifested in different forms in successive evolutionary stages. The human being, dwelling in the world of materialism and luxury, kept making the place for this illusion in the ever renewed and decorated rooms of his mind and spirit.

The art and literature are an effective challenge to this illusion, direct as well as indirect. Is our art and literature as well a challenge to this illusion? And if so, up to what level? This is the question the reply of which would be a litmus test for our cultural loftiness and literary greatness. For this process, an artist needs not obey his watcher or listener and a writer, his reader or listener. However our artist and writer would find a critic of his art and creativity and the measuring rod in himself.

30 November 2009

A literary organisation had organised a literature festival in the city today and I was also invited. I accepted the invitation and participated in the festival. Really telling, I felt very disgusted late because the programmes of the festival were merely cheap entertainment and nothing else.

It is doubtless that establishment of organisations is essential for the progress and development of art, language and literature. When we keep in consideration the role of famous national and international organisations, we strongly believe that collective struggle is needed for the progress and development of art, language and literature. Really telling, when we establish organisations for securing common aims, our condition worsens worse than politicians. We experience bias for granted. When we hold some post in the organisation, we feel as if we control the super power radar of a cartoon channel. We start flying in the imaginary skies. We perceive everything through the glasses of compromise and execute the same. It is where we doubt the suitability of the organisations. We have been watching it for decades. It is from the stages, we get with the blessing of the organisations. We announce that Kashmiri language is not inferior to any major language of the world in any field but the reality is that no one of us is ready to spend a single moment in harmonising the language with the contemporary informational and scientific challenges. It is not known why our organisers believe that our language can sustain till tomorrow on the basis of poetry and semi-mature, flat literary essays. May God forbid our language from the calamity that happened to Sanskrit! The reality is that our leaders of the organisations have the same illusion which the Sanskrit scholars had before six hundred years. Our organisations are successful in advertising but in practice we could not organise a movement for the creation of good literature rather we could not even initiate the same. Whatever was done for the creation of good literature, it was on an individual level. There is an unbridgeable difference between a movement and a riot. Either the organisers of these organisations have to think afresh about their suitability and significance and do a constructive role so that language and literature expands to new horizons as per contemporary challenges or for God's sake they should not riot and disturb one and all.

2 December 2009

Today in the evening, I have started writing a diary on the beautiful banks of river *Vitasta* in the *Rajbagh* area. Even during the chill times, the enthusiasm of flowing *Vitasta* vitalises one's heart and pleases it to sing.

This era is flowing like *Vitasta* as well. It is flowing from thousands of years, neither does it get tired nor does it stop to take rest. The passage of the era would continue in the times to come as well. We know the fact well that literature is a mirror to its era, the mirror in which we can see the face of the era in a better way. Literature too is flowing water. It changes its form every time and in every condition. We are aware of the literature of present time. Today's literature is different from the literature of yesterday and that of the day before yesterday in theme as well as in form. Tomorrow's literature would also be different from today's literature as it takes birth within the society. Tomorrow the condition of society would be different from what it is today. That is why the change would be observed in literature. In the future we would be more dependent on machines than we are at present. We have not only to change the lifestyle but we have to change mental attitudes also. There would be infinite alterations on political, social and economic spheres. The impact of westernisation would gradually diminish and the space would be filled by some Asian countries. Due to this the influence of nowadays third world would increase at international level and as such the languages of these countries would develop and progress. Yes, the languages which will be harmonised with computers would develop more and get upper status. Like other languages of the country our language too has the challenge of computerisation and digitisation before it. Our software engineers can help us in this and we have to tirelessly work for it from right now.

One more point is that the attitude of the changes in the social conditions augur that literature would be free from so many tangles in future. Unnecessary complexities would not be accepted for pedantic effects or for showing off of hollow literary greatness. Yes, there is a hope that literature would be more meaningful and sense full. The literature available on electronic media would be more significant than that present only in paper books. We will move out of this era of non- concern for each other and enter an era where we will need to think positively for each other. So for as in the present materialistic era where a man enticed with hollowness would suffocate in the run for perks and think for the values and ideals. After squeezing his self and spirit in tiny compartments the man would suffocate and he would break the binding borders and start thinking at humanitarian level. Sky would be his limit and he would grow greenery on the ground of thinking and multi coloured flowers would bloom there. The sweet smell of these flowers would find place in literature. The literature of the new era would advocate of human pleasure and all its branches would be clear and sacred. The conscience of a true litterateur can feel the pulse of tomorrow and his eyes can cross the borders of time and see tomorrow. Would this hope be against expectations that the roots of this type of tomorrow's literature should be nurtured from today?

21 April 2010

I was severely baffled from a number of days as I could not read anything. It is only by the virtue of reading that hundreds of tangles, of thought as well as action, have been detangled. It was really the bliss from the almighty lord that I chanced to look at a scientific book on galaxies in the market. I bought it and went straight home. I remained busy with the book the whole day. The heavenly journey refreshed me, my thoughts as well as my soul.

Reading and appreciating books is the most meaningful and auspicious characteristic of civilised life. It is something to be proud of and something to be jealous of. The advantages of book reading can be figured only when we shall make a difference between book readers and non readers. A non-reader is confined to his immediate world as per the time and era and he cannot get out of it unless he reads. As soon as he picks a book in his hand, the knot is untied and a door is opened to a new world. He meets one of the masters of literature of the world. The master of literature takes him far away from the immediate world to an imaginary one which he hadn't seen or comprehended till then. During this journey, new horizons of knowledge, new philosophy and new science are taken to meet him. It is because of this prospective journey that his conscience is cleansed and his perception of vision is widened. It is by the advent of this journey that fancy widens its area and the creation attains modesty. About the significance of the book reading, Chinese scholar and poet *Hiwang Shankoo* says, "A true scholar who hadn't read for three consecutive days admits that his speech isn't full of sense and he feels ashamed of himself in front of a mirror." Reading isn't a mechanical exercise but a delicate process which pleases ones' heart. Reading for attaining intellect hasn't any great value because reading while keeping such targets isn't pleasing and reading without pleasure hasn't any achievement. That is why it is said that reading for attaining personal attraction and imbibing speech with pleasure unveils worlds of expectations before a person and such a reading makes a man educated. In every era, only such a poet and litterateur has attained perfection and displayed the same, who was educated in this very sense. Not educated in a scholastic way.

The same thing can be said on a big canvas as well in this way: "The reading by which a soul attains sublimity and bliss is really essential. And what would he who hasn't read, say or write?" When we introspect, hopelessness waits desperately to embrace us. Either we have left reading or we have condemned ourselves of compartmentalised reading. And as such we are accustomed to the experience of this punishment. The non-melting ice of this habit has frozen our pen as well. This condition isn't conducive for our language and its literary health. That is why we should think and understand without any delay that we should read in every condition and reading should not be compartmentalised so that our literary future would not vanish.

24 May 2010

I read a critical essay in a literary magazine. The style of criticism left me dejected. While expressing his literary critical opinion he had downed to the personal criticism. He had commented on the essays of other critics as well. He opposed their unbiased and disinterested opinion so severely as if he took them ignorant. Our language still waits for such a credible critic who would dignify literary criticism.

A credible critic evaluates a literary work on the basis of particular principles and standards and finally reaches to conclusion. These principles and standards are his own and thus he can change his principles and standards for some particular writer; to expect so from a critic is injustice to him. Literature is destined to sacrifice the personal interests. And a critic isn't generally a desirable person in the eyes of writers. That is why romantic poet Keats had once told angrily about the critic, "Shoot this dog." Such an uncultured statement of a sensible poet arouses hundreds of questions. The fortune of true criticism isn't destined with this roughness and hatred only. When a serious writer emphatically expresses his grievances and antipathy against the art of literary criticism, then it becomes the responsibility of critic and criticism in particular and of literature in general to think over it. Although literature is the personal expression of the writer, it becomes public property once it is published or broadcast. The responsibility of a critic or reviewer isn't limited to this that he would analyse literary attitudes but he has to introduce readers to the world of literature and wholeheartedly reply to the questions related with literature. In addition to this, it is his responsibility as well to think over all the issues related to the cultural manifestations of literature. If this idea would be acceptable, the opposition to criticism would diminish itself as it would then be opposition to the whole cultural process which spreads from the creation of literature to its impact. In this way the opposition to the critic and criticism would mean opposition to cultural values.

However indifference to criticism isn't new, it is ages old. Yes, it is true that the critic is opposed more than the criticism is. When the majority of the creative writers seriously oppose, the need is felt to ascertain all the causes of this opposition and to think over it wisely.

One more point is that a good literary work is ordinarily multi-dimensional and impregnated with many levels of meaning and senses. It is rich in experiences due to lofty metaphorical construction. The ability of analysing the overall literary quality and significance of this type of literary creation is dependent on the approach of the critic. That is why it is needed that all the analysing tools of the critic should be sharp. On the basis of individual virtues, a good literary creation challenges a critic in finding those inherent qualities in it which distinguish it from all old creations and which are short in them. It is because of these inherent qualities that it attains creation and critic chooses it for appraisal. It is also true that only a few critics can stand on this challenge. Perhaps this might be why we can't find a good number of credible critics among thousands of writers.

30 September 2010

We all know that literature doesn't emerge from space but it is a long continuity of varied knowledge, situations, experiences and forms. If this literature is to be analysed or evaluated, it will be possible only when the analysis is done on the basis of knowledge, situations, experiences and forms. Today's literary creation is a trial of identifying and understanding such basic bewilderments which have become integral paradoxes of our life. These bewilderments are moral, ideological, cultural, religious, social, economic, political and of various other types. Until a critic recognises and comprehends these pressures and bewilderments, he cannot approach the spirit of the literary work nor can he evaluate it perfectly. In reality it is the duty of the critic to bridge the gap between the reader or listener and the writer. But it is equally true that for this work, a critic needs to have a reach to the literary work and be able to unravel the underlying meanings and sense of the creation and evaluate all the individual qualities of the creator. In addition to it, it is equally important to see how closely related the critic is to universal human affairs and attitudes. However, it is a truth as well that the critic would not be acquainted fully with these affairs and attitudes. He might be imprisoned in his fortes. This is observed mostly in such societies where there is a large difference between the contemporary global standards and the evolution in the education system. Due to this the society gets moulded by a non-harmonising paradigm and gets involved in a serious conflict. Our society isn't as well safe from the blow of such a conflict. It isn't a myth but a reality. But the voices have arisen against such a situation which seems to be a myth. The mental attitude conceiving the new human of the new world has stood against it and the whole-hearted trial to fill the vacuum which awkwardly subjugates our mental literary attitude from a number of decades is underway. In this context we cannot expect best results from the critic. However, we cannot acquit the critic from his responsibility on the basis of this condition. There are novel and fresh themes in the writings of the present era writer. But there is a need that the process of criticism should be systematically started only after analysing the organic unity of the creative pressures which the writer experiences. Only then justice can be done to the work of the writer. A critic should be aware about the cultural milieu and the ideological context in which a literary work has been created. In addition to it, a critic's ability to approach the ideological context of the writer results in a good analysis, appreciation and criticism. If the criticism is like this, it would be surely accepted as the literature of the first grade.

26 January 2012

Today is the 'Republic Day' of India. The talks of constitution making and of Indian democratic system were going on the whole day. When we talk about democracy, a question arises in our mind about how many democratic values have developed in our literary republic. The limitless freedom we enjoy in literature in conceiving experiences and expressing them and in journeying in the imaginary world isn't found elsewhere. Sometimes it is felt that we have not judiciously used this freedom, perhaps the literary values have weakened in effect. We have started using these values commercially. One more serious issue is that the literary standard has lost its importance in our eyes. A number of compromises have been made under the shadow of literature. Strange things have been produced. The implied classification of caste, region and faith and the literary discussions concerning them is a proof of it. It has also been observed that as soon as most of the writers get recognition as litterateurs, they publish whatever they like in the name of literature. Then they exploit the functional literary organisations for their personal interests and derail them from their goals.

The conflict between the editors of the literary magazines and the fiction writers or poets can be lengthened even to miles but we see it seems very difficult for an editor to walk for some paces for getting a quality poem or short story. We come to know after analysing the content of these literary magazines that the quality is not being taken care of due to easy-taking attitude or compromise on familiarity or face saving. In this way we deliberately lower the standard of literary journalism. It seems that nowadays the one and only aim of literary journalism is to publish a magazine and label oneself as editor. We acquire responsibilities once we attain a title or occupy a post but we fail to discharge the duties honestly. Very little quality literature is published in our literary magazines. The cause is not that the quality literature isn't produced but it is so because the editors of the magazines don't feel the need to move a few steps for quality literature. The literature which reaches to their door sills is included and as such a magazine of whatever quality is published. Due to this, the editor's recognition widens and so does his friend circle. This wave has produced an army of such writers who have found place in front lines despite their confined and amateurish literary expressions. Dozens of such writers have reached on to the stages and became skilled in different literary genres as a result of their continuing the system of compromises. This faulty attitude has impregnated our literary context. It is the duty of the serious writers and critics of our language to act instantly as doctors and treat the sick attitudes of our literature, so that we can have the ability to compete with the quality literature at national and international level.

25 February 2012

In the run for scientific advancement and economic progress of the contemporary materialistic world, man analyses everything by the rod of the pragmatic parameters. He decides about the applicability or inapplicability of the things on the basis of the results obtained as such. A question strongly arises in my mind: what is the need of a litterateur and what is the necessity of literature? Whole of the environment seems in opposition of the litterateur and the literature. The market conscience has strengthened this attitude as well. So many people are strongly working on setting the parameters linked to economic achievement for consolidating literary standards. The situation turned difficult as a result of the challenge of the technical means of communication from the very beginning of the twenty-first century. As if the words have lost credibility. We are facing some serious questions which are putting doubtful ecliptic shadows on the future of literature. The way the contemporary era and society, fact and fancy and idea and feeling change the conceptions of human beings, it is essential to see which image would emerge on the screen of literature. However, it is true that literature is one of the manifestations of the expression of the process of this change. So many means of expression are available nowadays. Future isn't completely uncertain and hidden nowadays. It isn't a mere fancy. The future is a living factor of our conscience. Although the future is not controllable by our five senses, it isn't out of the control of our insight. We have established connectivity with the future. Now we have to converse with the future which is based on technology. Some people say that a creative writer writes by the bliss of fancy and he writes something only on subjugating to the inner world. He hasn't to be subjugated to the external world and its knowledge like an educated litterateur. They hold that worldly knowledge can make the creative litterateur blunt. This is like what some writers say that when they read creations of others, their creative power is harmfully impacted. They may be true but it cannot be negated either that every new information, knowledge and discovery makes the fancy and the expression of the feeling more influential and multidimensional. When the writers will remain confined in their own worlds, the number of those who are interested in and read literature would diminish and the questions like what is literature would get prominence. It is so because the lover of literature goes close to it to understand this world.

Contemporary literature is almost free from all isms and movements. Nowadays the search for the new thought and ideology has begun, so that we can make literature a part of our life. The future is not possible without the literature. The idea of society can't be conceived in any form without literature.

9 July 2012

Today I was reading *Kshemendra* the whole day. I was impressed by his social consciousness. Till late in the night, I was analysing the revolutionary impact of influential literary creations of our times with reference to the readings of *Kshemendra*.

Literature is an unstoppable and untiring process of turning thought into expression, research into communication, and aesthetics into dialogue. Sometimes this movement is felt from inside to outside and at other times it is from outside to inside. Sometimes it dresses non-existent with the robes of existence and sometimes it makes concrete out of abstract. Don't we achieve greatness and farsightedness by witnessing the arguments of critics and eulogising them? Literature can't make a person better or make him a person of great ideas; however, it may enlighten his conscience and widen his feelings and emotions. To be a creative writer means to feel all those positive virtues in one self which are characteristic of a mother. A writer gives expression to feelings of man. The expression of feelings provides him sensibility. One of the ways of sensibility is developing curiosity for understanding the affairs and queries. These qualities are essential for a revolution. The revolutionary changes are impossible without them. Literature utilises that sensibility of society which later society uses as base for its ideological and spiritual individuality. This can be thought of in other ways as well. A common man endures his pain silently while a litterateur gives voice to his pain. This is due to this expression that this pain is recognised and identified as the pain of the whole of society. This is true that literature is a free expression of man and humanity.

Basically, this expression is not collective, it is individualistic. A man is always spiritually individualistic however he attains intellect and understanding only on becoming a part of society. Which is why, although not being a revolutionary, a litterateur is a sage who comprehends and expresses the conscience of his society. The voice of a litterateur is the voice of the age.

The preamble of the constitution of UNESCO declares: 'Since wars begin in the minds of men, it is in the minds only where the defences of peace must be constructed." And the mind is controlled by literature.

There are so many such instances in history that a book showed its era the way of revolution. It was after reading Shakespeare's play 'Richard Second', that Earl of Saxon lifted the flag of resistance against *Queen Elizabeth*. After reading Turgenev's Hunter's sketches, Tsar felt uncomfortable and he ordered the abolition of slavery. In the same way, Harriet Beecher Stowe's novel 'Uncle Tom's Cabin' played effective role in creating public opinion against the tradition of slavery. American president *Lincoln* had to say, "So this is the little lady who started this Great War!"

From how many difficult conditions and problems these writers had to pass through and it was only after that their sharp words provided the basis for the revolution. When a writer passes through such difficulties and discomforts, the eternal literature of universal appeal is created and it is due to that the writer after becoming a delineator of the intellect and conscience of his era, he enables himself to create new values. This contribution of literature is the greatest expectation of human existence.

15 September 2012

"Why do people read literature?", A young man asked me today. I replied to him after assessing his level of pursuance. He was satisfied; however, I remained contemplating on this for a long time. Why do people read literature? This question hasn't any fixed answer. Some people praise the ideational greatness of literature and advocate it as the essence of literature. The people who have working knowledge about the customs and traditions and multi dimensionality of literature or who aspire to have such knowledge are the real readers of literature. Then it doesn't matter whether they accept the literature either as a tool for social struggle or a means of self-realisation or merely a means of entertainment or anything else. Reading, especially reading literature is a personal conversation which remains going on between a writer and a reader. This reading becomes evaluative when there develops a relation of familiarity between the reader and the writer. Apparently reading seems to be a one way process, that the writer says something and a reader listens to that and consequently grasps something from it. In this process, the give and take of relation is not visible. It seems reality on seeing superficially, however it is not a truth for a serious reader. A real reader is always an inventor and creator in himself. He doesn't merely approach and appreciate the clear and pure statements of the writer but he tries to comprehend and expose all those abstract and delicate figures and possibilities which are absorbed in the creation during the miraculous moments of the creative process. He gets such hidden meaning and information from the creation of which the creator is not certain about. A famous Sanskrit Quote is that a poet creates only a poem, the sky of this creation is journeyed only by a sage-critic who is able to fly above the surface.

Purposeful and serious reading is possible only when a writer provides an effective opportunity for this. As some basic mental and spiritual attitudes are beneficial for a writer to create literature, in the same way there are some advantageous characteristics for a good reader. A good reader of literature is one who reads with the emotion of humbleness and who enjoys reading and gets something to practise. Reading literature is to dive into the sea of human life and get models of some shining diamonds and pearls from the resources of experience. One of the greatest scholars of the world of literature, *Abinav Gupta* says that until the poetry appreciating illuminated self awakens the inner senses and harmonises them with the nature and characteristics of poetry, he would not get access to the poetical fancy and enjoy the expression of the poetry. It is also true that only after reading literature we can say how to read it and what to read. Whatever we read, we would keep the inner senses of being awake and harmonise them with the nature and characteristics of literature, so that we can have an approach to the spirit of the literature.

1 January 2013

The environment, in which we live, has given us a number of paradoxes and tensions. Sometimes I feel very restless thinking over these paradoxes and tensions.

For a sensible writer this environment is full of paradoxes and tensions and it is the basic principle of the development of conflict that these paradoxes and tensions would increase day by day. These paradoxes and tensions are primordially hidden in the written form from ages and these are also present in the literature of each era. However the only difference is that these paradoxes and tensions are manifest and decisive nowadays. In the world of creation, a writer is directly linked to the result of these conflicts and dejections and is perhaps destined that he would cross over this sea of conflict, paradox and tension and while doing this create his work. In contemporary literature the contemporaneous discourse and harmonising tools have been so centric that the relation with present reality has turned colourless, superficial and weak. The contemporary complexities and the mature approach demands that within the historical and social conscience and out of it that human honour and relation be preferred which has lost in the vagaries of time. In the contemporary situation it is only the intellect and vision of recognition of the litterateur that can pass through the tension, paradox and conflict and can meet, give form to and set identity of such a person who is primordial inspiration of all the arts and cultural faiths. The decision of applicability, suitability and meaningfulness of not only the contemporary but of the literature of all times should be based on seeing as to which level this human relation and the intensity of pleasure is present in it. It is also to be seen what the human, who is delineated in it, looks like. It means the closer the world of literature is to the human world, the more suitable and qualitative it is. The literature in which this relation is missing and in which the timely requirements are adorned with the flying words, that literature gives an illusion of being contemporaneous. In most of the literature of our times the hazy storm of unstable words has faded the figure of human beings. But the reality is that the grasp of truth is loosened with the words. This is the issue which the contemporary litterateurs have to ponder over so that its solution would guide.

George Steiner once wrote, "When the words in the city are full of savagery and lies, nothing speaks louder than the unwritten poem." The power of this unwritten poem is like the chirping of those birds that have been consoling the heart and mind since thousands of years ago to present times. In the same way our literature is impregnated by savage queries. The only hope, in this context, is of such an unwritten literature which will be written in future and the solutions of the savage queries would come forth. This literature would be an ambassador of the festivity of our ability, suitability and applicability.

———❧———

6 January 2013

In every person there certainly exists more or less some other person who not only dreams or feels the deepening inspiration for the sake of principles for some moments but who suddenly forgets himself in recollecting the memories of the past and loses his mental peace. It is the same person who attains mental solace and pleasure in the intoxication of the imagination of the future. Different faculties of art and literature become directly helpful in every possibility of widening of the individual personality of a person. The greatest need of the tasteful literature is that it would solace the mental and spiritual discomfiture of the person who is in pursuit of possibilities and who dreams for the better.

Literature sharpens our fancy and imagination and gives a direction to our longing for new experiments and curiosity for knowing the unknown. The thought process of literature empowers us for the struggle of life and for harmonising the cultural unities.

Some days before in a literary discussion some renowned litterateurs advocated that literature and its structure should be made understandable to the common person. This, in other words, means that the soup of good literature is concentrated. It is to be mixed with water and diluted. The thin designed thread used for its structure is to be replaced by thick woollen thread. The result would talk itself.

18 January 2013

Sometime before a seminar was held in the University of Kashmir which was titled as "Global values in literature". Today I recollected the seminar all of a sudden. The seminar and its title gave me a question as well to ponder over and the question is "what can we call healthy literature?"

After so many days I felt the need to express my opinion to myself. Literature isn't mere projection of the background of the litterateur but it is the name of the life's heart beat in which there are hundreds of springs of pain and infinite autumns of pleasure. When this beating life becomes the kiss of the tearful eyes and holy incantation of the thirsty lips, the creator of the universe makes effective sprinkle from the holy urn of pity. This sprinkle ablutes the earthly creators of the words and the literature comes into being and it makes and adores the era. This is the literature which provides us pleasure and bliss and quenches the thirst of centuries in moments. It is due to this literature which makes us capable of sojourning to the different sides of earth and skies.

The healthy literature is a representative of pious and undefiled values and such literature is free from the bondage of flat ideologies. The literature of international standard or global literature is not confined to some set ideology but it is the literature of aesthetics and universality. It is such an aesthetic glance which isn't intervened by any glasses of bias, jealousy or compartmentalisation. It has such a capability that the complete existence of creation comes before the eyes. Every such attitude which augurs new possibilities for expression is acceptable for the global literature. The literature of global quality does not accept any sort of compartmentalisation.

There is a need to upbringing such traditions in literature which have been put on back burner by narrow-mindedness and jealousy. We have to put off the veil of narrow-mindedness from such illuminating universal traditions. For the illumination by new challenges and new enlightenment of literature we have to solemnly resolve to stand against the darkness of ignorance. Perhaps only after that a way can be found to the creation of such universal or global literature which will dignify our language and our creative potential.

******

On the one hand our language is destined with literary loftiness but simultaneously Kashmiri literary scenario is challenged by disruptive factors and cheap compromises from a number of decades. On one hand the literary hollowness is honoured and on the other hand there is pomp and show of the statements without arguments and of baseless literary verdicts. A number of young writers and some senior writers are involved in this unhealthy attitude of literary brokerage. When at the national and international level the litterateurs are busy with the application of new thoughtful themes and latest attitudes, we are hung by these negative capabilities and attitudes.

No literary movement can stand long on the crutches of compromises. Time passes in vain and so does our literary ability go waste. The greed for getting timely benefits is already disadvantageous for oneself in the long run, but it is fatal for a language. We should immediately take to lime light those positive dimensions which we have voluntarily kept hidden so that our literary environment may get rid of the shadow of the hollowness.

30 March 2013

Today I was provided a chance by a private college to have a literary talk with its students. The students asked me a number of questions about the art of translation. I enjoyed the talk with the students. It is beyond doubt that our new generation is sensible and intelligent. It only needs to be given a direction. The things which I shared with the students were summed up in my diary.

The globalisation (I am personally comfortable with universalization) has taken not only different regions or individuals close but it has taken different philosophies, spiritual ideologies, faiths, cultures, languages and literatures of these languages also very close to one another. The contemporary communicative revolution has taken us from locality to universality. In this background the translator's significance has been recognised. The translation became such a bridge which abridged the linguistic and cultural ravines and gaps and by the advent of which we became able to approach each other's sensibility. When a poem or a short story journeys from one language to another, from start to end it has to pass through an area which instead of belonging to both of them does not belong to either of them practically. It is just like the No Man's Land between the two sovereign states. Every translator has to pass through this non estate area and it is a challenge for him.

For translation, the broadmindedness of a translator is more important than his mastery of languages. The important part of this broadmindedness is the ability to fly in the sky of expression of those of which the translations are being done. It is also important that the relation between the wings and the sky to fly be mature enough. If a translator is not familiar with people for whom this toil and struggle is done, then the relation with the translation cannot be developed smoothly by a reader. The work of another language is naturally strange for a reader and to change this strangeness into familiarity is the job of the translator. When the translator succeeds in discharging this responsibility satisfactorily, he can raise his head in dignity and stand shoulder to shoulder with the original writer.

By turning the flow of expression, culture and meaningful dialogue from the other language to one's own language or translating the same from one's own language to another language, the translator builds such a bridge on travelling which we succeed in filling various linguistic, cultural, ideological, spiritual and literary gaps. And the question which emerges here is whether the translator has any place after the completion of the process of translation. Is he present anywhere between the reader and writer? Of course, he is there. The underwater supporting pole which bears the weight of the bridge which had been built from one bank of the channel to another, which cannot be seen in rushing channel, is that translator upon whose shoulders the bridge of communication exists. He suits to be in water concealed from the eyes. He should not be perceptible to the eyes as well. It is only then that a reader will feel that he is reading the original work and appreciate the reading as well.

1 April 2013

The present era always stands against the past and contemplates on its condition. The past era puts forward its experiences to the present and such becomes a mile stone for it. Sometimes the past becomes a means of identity of the present. How strong is this relation of identity? It is a matter of concern and curiosity for individuals, races, castes, nations and states at each level. When danger to the identity is felt, voluntarily the struggle for the revival of the traditions is undertaken. However it is true only when we find the human values, feelings and ideas in the traditions valuable and applicable for the present. Otherwise the past becomes a heavy load for the present and by it the barrenness and impotence of the present seems to be increasing.

In reality, before developing the cultural values imbibed from the tradition on modern lines, it is essential to identify and recognise their human and humanitarian belongingness. This identification can be done only on the cultural basis and not on the basis of religion, caste or language. We can go on a long journey only on the vehicles of universal human relations.

****

I just finished reading Kashmiri Sanskrit poet *Kshemendra's* famous book *'Kala Villas'*. The unknown features of the history of the eleventh century Kashmir unveiled before me. The literature of an area is an essential and standard source for compiling the history of different branches of life of that era. Literature of an era cannot remain uninfluenced by its contemporary conditions, events and their resulting psychological impact. That is why whenever the real face of an era is to be found, it is searched through the mirror of literature.

Literature of an era comes into existence, progresses and develops under the influence of conditions of that era. It is true that the present conditions of an era are not directly delineated by the standard and quality literature of the era. However the timely conditions are figured in such a way after concretising them in the kiln of universality that makes the literature not only relative to its contemporary themes and conditions but also makes it suitable for the conditions and nature of every era. This is the basis of creative literature. Otherwise, literature becomes a newspaper of its era. Such a literature faces the same fate after its era which the newspaper of today faces the next morning. Without baking it in the kiln when we write directly on the present conditions and without inducing creative and aesthetic quality in our write ups, we produce ephemeral and a newspaper type of literature which is little aged and incredulous.

6 April 2013

Nowadays a number of allegations are set on contemporary literature produced by young writers. The same thing happened today in our city too. A senior and elder litterateur said that the young literature of our language is not harmonising with our ethos and culture. A number of young writers present there challenged it. There was a sharp argument.

The matter subsided with very difficult. It is not the matter of the literature of our language only. It is an issue in most of the languages of the world. The young literature is challenged by the allegations of being irresponsible, iconoclastic and derailed. All these allegations are natural as this problem is faced by every new generation. Whenever new ideas and new mental attitudes, new values and changes erupt in the literary scenario or whenever new possibilities come to existence, the generation cling to the age old rites, rituals and traditions does not accept the changes and raises its voice against it.

In the present ruthless conditions and in the steel claws of ugly, disfigured beings, it is difficult for our new generation even to breathe. Meanwhile this generation has to endure utterly useless, unsuitable, awkward and illogical rituals and traditions. However time plays its role. Nowadays when the under-step ground flees away and the rushing water of the present era erodes the land of the foundation with it, how much suitable are the mental attitudes based on the fundamentalist approach of the tradition? The answer to this question is not hidden from anybody. On accepting the already set values in totality, everybody finds himself on the ever changing and ever hanging base and feels himself insecure. And that is why the young generation has to find new values for itself and as such it becomes a necessity to modify the traditional value system. The way of the young literary creation is very difficult because it has to level the land for itself. It is very easy to tread on the old ways however these old and already treded ways have lost their significance in the contemporary changes. That is why it is necessary to build new ways and face new dangers and difficulties. This difficult work is the responsibility of our young writer.

To analyse the traditional hope and faith by the personal paradigm and subsequently to forget and leave them or to keep them fresh in memory and nurture them in self and simultaneously enduring the difficulties and finding new truths and realities and while doing that, being ready for any sacrifice. All these things are not easy. To keep one-self updated with the current era and to develop one's mental set up on the rational scientific basis, our young writer is facing all these challenges. He is destined to pass through the ruthless and agonising system of mental attitudes and perspectives. The more our young writer faces these challenges and writes with consistency, the more credibility his writings will attain.

The word "young" is representative of mental freshness and not of the age in terms of years. In the contemporary era the young generation, which gives wider meanings to the time, can create the more honest literature. That is why we have great expectations from the young literature in the contemporary era.

9 APRIL 2013

My conscience satiated and mind refreshed today after reading the spiritually exalted and sublimated *'Dhama Pada'*. On the one hand I felt as if I was listening to some divinely confidential secret from a sage and on the other hand I was as much aesthetically pleased as I get on reading verses of *Lala Ded* (Laleshwari). Famous thinker and philosopher Simone Weil says that the significance of the religious and spiritual life is based on whether it illuminates and enlightens its surroundings. This brief statement is a key as well as an analytical tool for searching such a truth dearth of which and the resultant restlessness is felt in our literature for decades. The truth is that a revolution or a change is possible only when the man is conceptualised and realised as the centre.

Such an idea of the human level does neither disable the perception of the social beings nor does it remain aloof from the illuminating yet afflicting feeling of alignment with the vast universe. The truth is that there is no alternative to this idea and perception. For our ease, we talk about the financial man or the political man at certain times. To envelope such an ease of research with the ideological jealousy and bias is not only jilting one's own self but also to save one's own self from the difficult issues of human condition. To negate the human spiritual thirst in the name of opposing different faiths or delinking the spiritual thirst from the social experiences of the human, both these conditions are opposed to the conception that human is the centre of the universe. Both these conditions which apparently give an illusion of leading to diverse directions in reality lead to only one destination and the destination is the state of partial fitness. On reaching this destination either we feel proud even on our disability and boast about it or we struggle to go back to that state of feeling where to leave it seemed essential to us. But is this sense and feeling of perfection perceived by everyone easily or does it need abstinence and hard work? The blank space which is present at the end of this question is that of a true writer before whom there is an issue of such a creation which makes every culture and civilisation to have a dialogue with others as per their capacity. Carrying the bag full of glow worms of silence, this writer voyages the haunting places of darkness. The more our Kashmiri writer succeeds in making dialogue with others and the more he crosses the darkness, the more our language would be exalted and the writer dignified.

18 APRIL 2013

One of our contemporaries published his poetry anthology some days before. Two new genres are introduced in the anthology. Despite being of an unusual and different nature and attitude, these two genres are very pleasing and beautiful. I talked with a number of persons having knowledge of prosody about this contribution. Most of them praised the contribution however some senior writers raised their eyebrows.

Whenever a new genre originates in literature and attains its form and content, the writers who are hung on to the traditional genres look down upon it or take it for granted otherwise they launch a movement against it and struggle against its evolution. Instead of it the writers of new genres are enthusiastic and they voluntarily overlook and leave behind the traditional genres. They use their power and ability in making others accept that the new genres are the representatives of the new era. Whoever has studied the origination and historical evolution of the modern poem, novel, short story or play, he would be better known for the fact that whenever the new generation tried to give form and shape to a new genre, they were opposed vehemently. However we cannot either negate the historical fact that the ability and intellect of the young writers overcome this opposition. The young writers filled the treasure of literature with the new genres by their quality and standard creative potential. We cannot keep the young generation aloof from making new and meaningful experiments as they do in other spheres of life. If we do this, not only the development of literature but whole human progress would come to halt. As our body ever needs new blood, in the same way the body of society as well as the body of literature needs new ideas, new thoughts, new references and new artistic hopes and inspirations. Modernisation recreates new life and influence in society and literature. It makes the new generation meaningful and ambitious. The cause of the fame and opposition of brief short story is the same that the young short story writers have made brief short stories their means of creative potential from the last two decades and they have made tireless efforts for gaining its acceptance and recognition in literary circles. Such new experiments were made in the poems and other literary genres as well but they were not as successful as in the case of short stories. It was only the brief short story that could attain recognition for its successful existence and changed the whole situation of the short story.

****

Concerning literature, it has been emerging as a matter of discussion nowadays (however in a concealed way) that the present era writer's relation with his social environment and his readers has weakened and his discourse has ceased. This situation has evèn a fatal effect on his creative potential as well. Due to weakening of the relation of discourse, the expression of pain by the contemporary writer seems to be a mere individualistic cry which is overlooked by his era and is taken for-granted. This condition is not conducive for the quality and wellness of literature. That is why it is the need of the hour to search for a functional base of thought on which a suitable dialogue can be initiated between the writer and the reader. We can light the lamps of broad-mindedness and expressiveness in the darkness of conservation, bias and jealousy which are surrounding us and by doing this we can reconnect the broken relations once again. This is the biggest challenge before contemporary writers.

———∞———

9 May 2013

Some days before a senior writer gave me his new book for reading. There are a number of linguistic, literary, historical, and cultural articles in it. While giving me the book he complained that I never review or comment on his publications. It is due to his complaint that today I read a few articles from the book. I was utterly bored reading these so-called research articles.

Apparently, a big platoon of so-called linguists, literary and cultural scholars has emerged around us. They have proved their existence by writing hundreds of articles. Most of the linguists who talk on the important issues of our language are those who haven't any knowledge about the *Dardic-Khowar* group of languages. Neither they know Sanskrit nor, they have any proficiency in Persian. They even don't know anything about the cultural background, the knowledge of which is essentially required before talking on these issues. In the same way so many cultural matters have been presented by the writers arbitrarily in their own way. Most of the matter presented in these articles has erupted from within the writer and not from any logical and observed sources.

We are fortunate that our forefathers have left behind big treasures of knowledge of different subjects for us. However, we don't know why it does not seem important to us to identify and recognise our illuminating past? We are accustomed to accept and appreciate the hollowness that is too full of noise. That is why senseless articles are presented before us. The articles without any beginning, body or conclusion, lead to nowhere but are a haphazard collection of words full of noise signifying nothing. We prepare lists of word similarities and issue linguistic verdicts merely on their bases. We think with ourselves for a while and declare that "A" does not exist as a poet. Similarly, without any logic and proof we say that this poem is not written by "A", it belongs to "B". One bursts into laughter on listening to these stories. When we want to know some basic things about a topic from a writer who has written a number of research papers on it, to our utter astonishment he does not know the basics of the field. Our scholars haven't read even a single book out of dozens available in the social and cultural context of the eleventh century despite that they are busy in the project of rectifying and editing the text of the poet of that century, *Lala Ded*. Without knowing of yesterday, while basking in the sun they make a foolish act of relating a village named *Sunner* with a sunny day. Not only this, they don't hesitate in declaring that this is a new approach to history. We are not better than them. We listen to this gossip and clap to please them.

All this is not a healthy attitude for our collective identity. We call Kashmir as Little Iran. But we are not suitable to recompense or indemnify the cultural behaviour of the Iranians if they lose it. They are very conscious about their cultural heritage and they would never accept any such imperfection which we normally dignify. By compromising in the cultural and literary matters, we are continuously clipping our stature and one day this trend of action and attitude would turn our existence into non-existence.

Satish Vimal is a representative Kashmiri, Hindi and Urdu writer. His twenty-two books have been published till now. In addition, he has contributed to more than two dozen anthologies and literary and cultural projects of the distinguished organisations and universities. A poet, short story writer, critic, literary aesthetician, cultural crusader and a translator of repute, *Satish* has been awarded by premier organisations and Ministries of India for his literary contribution including Sahitya Akademi, Central Hindi Directorate, Ministry of I&B (Govt of India) for his contribution to literary journalism & creative writings, J&K Academy of Art Culture & Languages, Governor of J&K and many prominent literary organisations of India. His writings have been translated into numerous Indian and foreign languages. *Vimal* has translated selected writings of fifty contemporary world poets into Kashmiri & Hindi. His research and evaluative articles have been published in leading journals and periodicals.

(e-mail: satishvimal@gmail.com)

Ashraf Raavi writes in Kashmiri, Urdu and English languages. His fields of writing are poetry, fiction, Children literature and literary criticism. He is a lecturer in School Education Department in J&K (India). A post graduate in political science and English with a diploma in teaching English, he is adept in Translation as well. His Published books include English Translation of Kashmiri short stories entitled THE CONSCIENCE OF KASHMIR and a book of literary criticism in Kashmiri entitled GONA SAVI GONMAATH.

The writer is a regular contributor to Radio literary broadcasts in Kashmir. He is also associated with J&K Academy of Art, Culture and Languages. (e-mail: ashrafraavi@gmail.com)

———✿———